The Color of Calm

90 Coloring Pages to Bring You Peace of Mind

Workman Publishing · New York

Workman
Workman Publishing
Hachette Book Group, Inc.
1290 Avenue of the Americas
New York, NY 10104
workman.com

Workman is an imprint of Workman Publishing, a division of Hachette Book Group, Inc. The Workman name and logo are registered trademarks of Hachette Book Group, Inc.

Design by Reagan Ruff

The publisher is not responsible for websites (or their content) that are not owned by the publisher.

Workman books may be purchased in bulk for business, educational, or promotional use. For information, please contact your local bookseller or the Hachette Book Group Special Markets Department at special.markets@hbgusa.com.

ISBN 978-1-5235-2931-5

First Edition March 2024
Printed in the United States of America on responsibly sourced paper.
10 9 8 7 6 5 4 3 2

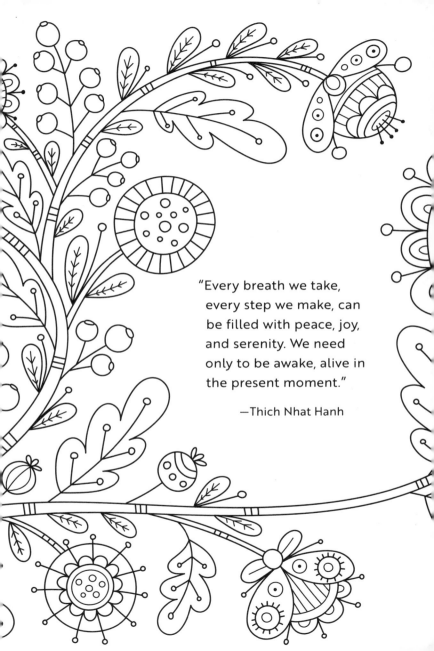

"Every breath we take, every step we make, can be filled with peace, joy, and serenity. We need only to be awake, alive in the present moment."

—Thich Nhat Hanh

Introduction

In our busy and chaotic world, it's more important than ever to take the time to wind down, quiet your mind, and relax. In other words, make space in your schedule for the simple and nourishing activities that bring you serenity and comfort. This coloring book is a visual love letter to the spirit of calm—you'll discover detailed patterns, soothing images, and unique shapes—all meant to inspire you to find peace in everyday life.

Pick up a colored pencil, crayon, or marker—whatever you have on hand will do—and let your imagination run free. Take a deep breath and remember that you deserve this time to yourself. Perfection isn't the goal. You don't even need to color inside the lines. Allow yourself to get lost in the intricacy of the art on the following pages and the comforting sound of pencil on paper. Find your calm, *your* way.

About the Illustrator

Yuliia Bahniuk is an illustrator and surface pattern designer from Ukraine, currently living in India with her husband, Rohan, and their cat, Toothless. Nature is one of her biggest inspirations, and she is an avid bird-watcher. She strives to spread awareness about the environment through her illustrations, which are often rooted in Ukrainian culture and filled with traditional ornaments and ancient symbols that create unique patterns. Her work has appeared in children's books, magazines, board games, apparel, home decor, and other products. To see more of her work, visit yuliiabahniuk.com.